THE GEMINI PERSONALITY

May 22 to June 21

A Portrait by Roy McKie

Collins: London and Glasgow

Gemini people have sex appeal,

are witty

and inventive.

They can't stand waiting,

love clothes

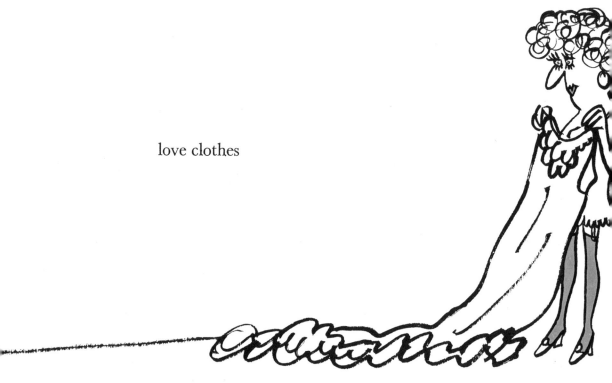

and are good salesmen.

They are observant

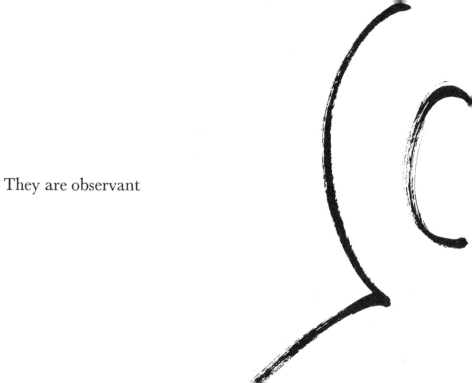

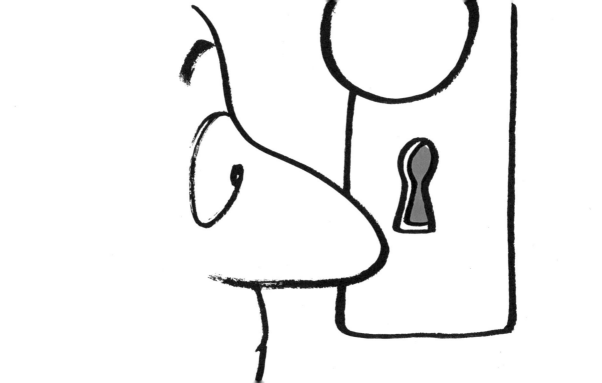

and their moods swing from one extreme

to the other.

They smoke too much,

are apt to read the last page of a book first

and are frequently underweight.

They are flirtatious,

easily distracted

and apt to leave you with the check.

They are tremendous talkers,

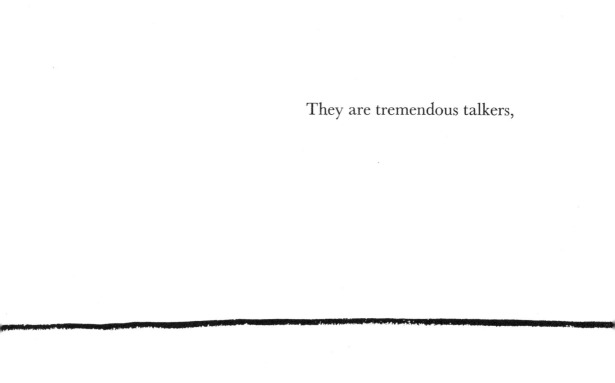

have a taste for knickknacks

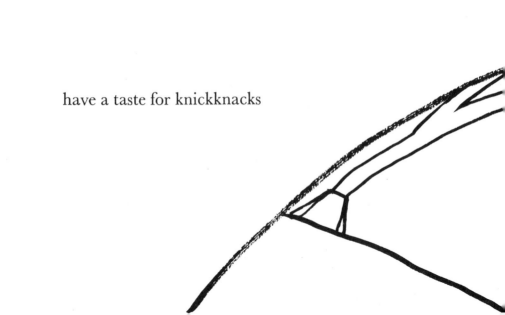

and occasionally don't honour deep commitments.

They marry often,

are glamorous,

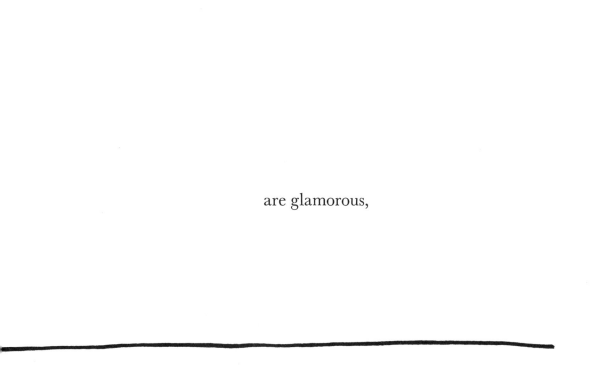

sparkling